Simon Stephens

Rage

methuen | drama

LONDON • NEW YORK • OXFORD • NEW DELHI • SYDNEY

METHUEN DRAMA
Bloomsbury Publishing Plc
50 Bedford Square, London WC1B 3DP, UK
1385 Broadway, New York, NY 10018, USA
29 Earlsfort Terrace, Dublin 2, Ireland

BLOOMSBURY, METHUEN DRAMA and the Methuen Drama logo
are trade marks of Bloomsbury Publishing Plc

First published in Great Britain 2018
Reprinted 2022

Cover design by Toby Way
Photography by Joel Goodman

This version of the text went to print before the end of rehearsals
and may differ slightly from the version performed.

No rights in incidental music or songs contained in the work are
hereby granted and performance rights for any performance/presentation
whatsoever must be obtained from the respective copyright owners.

All rights whatsoever in this play are strictly reserved and application
for performance etc. should be made before rehearsals by professionals and
by amateurs to Casarotto Ramsay & Associates Ltd, Waverley House,
7–12 Noel Street, London W1F 8GQ (agents@casarotto.co.uk).
No performance may be given unless a licence has been obtained.

A catalogue record for this book is available from the British Library.

ISBN: PB: 978-1-3501-1075-5
ePDF: 978-1-3501-1076-2
ePub: 978-1-3501-1077-9

Series: Modern Plays

Typeset by Country Setting, Kingdown, Kent CT14 8ES
Printed and bound in Great Britain

To find out more about our authors and books visit www.bloomsbury.com
and sign up for our newsletters.

Introduction

In December of 2015 my friend and long-term collaborator
Sebastian Nubling asked me to write a play for him. He
wanted me to write a response to the new play by Nobel
Laureate Elfriede Jelinek that he would be directing at
Hamburg's Thalia Theater. Her play, *Wut* (which loosely
translates as 'fury') was a text some hundred and twenty pages
in length. It was an imaginative reconstruction of the massacre
carried out by Islamist terrorists at the headquarters of the
satirical magazine *Charlie Hebdo* in Paris earlier that year.

I love Jelinek's writing. I love her eloquence and formal explosion
and linguistic energy and moral honesty. I asked Sebastian if
I could read the play in an English translation. He told me
I couldn't because there was no English translation of the play.
He asked me if could I make a response to it anyway. He
asked me if I could write it by April of the following year.

It seemed a difficult task. To write a play in response to another
play that I couldn't read. A formally exploratory play defined
by an examination of rage.

In three months.

Sebastian suggested I could just think about my own ideas of
rage. What does rage mean to me? Where have I encountered
it? Where has it moved me? When have I felt it? I liked his
questions, and certainly, in the first year of David Cameron's
Tory government and the final months before the Brexit
referendum that would end his brief, absurd tenure, there was
much about Britain that was making me furious and a sense
of increasing anger throughout the country. But nevertheless
I didn't have an anchor. I needed something to steady my
anger if I was going to be able to make something for him.

And then, in the first weeks of 2016 I saw Joel Goodman's
photographs of New Year's Eve around Well Street in
Manchester. The most celebrated of his photographs became
an international sensation. It went viral on the internet. It

depicted several events in one moment. A young man is arrested by four police officers. The arrest or its force causes the horror of a girl who is watching it happen. Others in the area stand to watch. Meanwhile a man in blue, apparently nearly comatose by alcohol, lies in the middle of the road and reaches to a nearby beer bottle on the street.

The photograph had a formal poise to it. Many observed that it accorded to Leonardo da Vinci's model of the golden median. They found in the photograph a classical cogency applied to a scene of alcoholic carnage and horror, violence and anger.

I loved the photograph. I loved it for its elegance and its form. It was beautifully lit. It also seemed to capture something that I recognised in Britain at that time. It seemed to capture the sense of dislocation and disorder of a country that, as it voted to dismantle its own economic security by leaving the EU, seemed to be committing a kind of suicide. It captured completely what I felt when I considered rage or fury in my country at that time.

I found out that the photograph was one of a series. There were thirty-one photos in total. Each slightly different in perspective or tone, but in their entirety they seemed to offer a startling insight into my experience of Britain then. In their capturing of the drunken fury and in the way they seemed charged by sexual desire, by violence, by hatred and love alike, they seemed to crystallise the feelings I was exploring as I reached to respond to the Jelinek play for Sebastian. I rang him to tell him that I had an idea for a play.

My idea was this. Every day in March, a month that I noticed had thirty-one days in it, I would write a response to one of Goodman's photographs. Unusually for me I wouldn't plan the scenes. I would try not to look ahead to the next day's photograph or edit or chart their relationships in any way. I would just write, for an hour or, so my response to what I saw.

And every day I would email Sebastian a new scene. And so throughout March I would build up a collage of scenes and he would have a new play, a play that in the most indirect way possible responded to Jelinek's *Wut*. A chaotic disordered exploration of rage for a culture of chaotic disorder.

He loved the idea. I wrote the scenes. With his dramaturg Julia Lochte, he and I shaped the collage into a kind of order that made dramaturgical sense of its counterpoint to *Wut*. He directed it at the Thalia in Hamburg at the end of 2016. As I write it is still running there.

Over the last year or so I have looked at the play with actors from the Royal Welsh College of Music & Drama. I wanted to find an order or a shape to my collage of my own. I wanted, effectively, to make my own version of the collage. To find a cogent dramaturgy of my own that meant it can exist independently of the Jelinek.

That version is what is published here.

As I read the scenes, scenes born out of an instinctive exploration of a country in fragmentation, I noticed recurring themes and atomised figures I could blend into characters. It is important to me that few of the figures have names; they are, I think, manifestations of feeling or tone rather than imagined human beings. Nights like the night on which Goodman saw humanity fracture. Through their booze and chaos and pure, distilled anger, they are events of dehumanisation. I wanted to capture that.

The noise of the imminence of the Brexit vote seems to hum under the scenes. I think it is that imminence, born as it was, out of inchoate anger and a need to tear down structures, that is captured in some of the violence of the play. It is certainly captured in the racial fear and hatred some of the figures articulate. I thought at the time of writing, and still feel to a degree, that much of the anger that led to the decision to leave the European Union of trade agreements, was a product of racism. I think Nigel Farage, who led the campaign to leave the

EU, is motivated by racism as much as he is by greed. I think his campaign celebrated his racist sentiments. He kindled irrational patriotism and exaggerated latent fears of movement of people through borders. My sense of that racism is captured in some of the language and images articulated here.

I make no apology for that language or those images. I am aware that it can make for distressing reading or unsettling dramatic speech. I think it is important for art, on occasion, to distress or unsettle. I think the job of dramatists is to create an imaginary psychosis on their stages so that their audiences can experience and explore psychosis in auditoria as a means of having to explore it less in their life.

The psychosis of *Rage* is fractured and sexually needy, incoherent, drunken, sometimes racist and terrified. I think it is so because that state is what Goodman captured in his photographs on that New Year's night, and it is what I recognised as being a defining tone of the country I lived in as it plunged its way towards economic self-destruction at the start of that year.

I would like to think that state of fractured psychosis in Britain has passed or is passing. In that sense *Rage* would become quickly irrelevant. I don't think it is though. I think, if anything, it is getting more overt and will continue to do so as one of the consequences of our almost unavoidable economic catastrophe to come.

Rage

Author's Note

These scenes are set in a major British city on New Year's Eve in the second decade of this millennium.

They were inspired by the photographs of Joel Goodman taken for the *Manchester Evening News* in Manchester on New Year's Eve 2015–16 and published in the *Manchester Evening News*.

They were written, originally, to counterpoint Elfriede Jelinek's play *Wut* (Rage) in Sebastian Nubling's production of that play at the Thalia Theater, Hamburg, in autumn 2016.

The character called 'Ralph Lauren' is NOT actually the American fashion designer Ralph Lauren, but rather somebody wearing clothes that the company the designer formed made.

The world premiere of *Rage* took place at the Thalia Theater, Hamburg, on 16 September 2016 with the following cast and creative team.

Cast

Kristof Van Boven
Marina Galic
Julian Greis
Franziska Hartmann
Marie Löcker
Karin Neuhäuser
Sven Schelker
Sebastian Zimmler

Creative Team

Director   Sebastian Nübling
Design   Eva-Maria Bauer
Costume Design   Pascale Martin
Music   Lars Wittershagen
Lighting   Jan Haas
Dramaturgy   Julia Lochte

The UK premiere of *Rage* took place in the Bute Theatre at the Royal Welsh College of Music & Drama, Cardiff, Wales, on Wednesday 28 November 2018. It was produced and performed by members of the College's Richard Burton Company, with the following cast and creative team.

Cast

Amesh Edireweera
Finnian Garbutt
Samuel Gosrani
Ruby Hartley
Peter Heenan
Abbie Hern
Emily John
Alyse McCamish
Yasemin Ozdemir
Grace Quigley
Alex Wanebo
Garyn Williams

Creative Team

Director Elle While
Set and Costume Designer Al Sadler
Lighting Designer Jasmine Williams
Composer Lincoln Barrett
Sound Designer Charlie Foran
Movement Director Frances Newman
Associate Director Sion Daniel Young
Voice Work/Dialect Coach Rhian Cronshaw

Characters

Brother
Sister
Ralph Lauren
Girl Who Sparkles
Grinning Boy
Redhead Boy
Police 1, *male*
Police 2, *Michael*
Police 3, *male*
Police 4, *female*
Passenger
Driver
Girl With No Shoes
Girl With Trainers
Woman Who Can See Under The World
Woman With A Bag
Man With Sideburns
Woman In A Flowery Dress
Helicopter Boy
Man In Blue
Vijay
Maria
Woman With A Tiara
The Woman

Sister   Are you excited?

Brother   I'm fucking excited.

Sister   Me too.

Brother   I can barely breathe with excitement.

Sister   What do you want to do?

Brother   Everything.

Sister   Everything?

Brother   All of it.

Sister   Where do you want to go?

Brother   I want to go to all the places.

Sister   You're funny.

Brother   I want to go to all of the places and meet everybody. Talk to all of them.

Sister   Dance with them all.

Brother   Film them all dancing. I want to drink all the drinks and eat all the food.

Sister   Take all the drugs.

Brother   We can't take drugs.

Sister   We can.

Brother   We're only fourteen.

Sister   Are you scared or something?

Brother   Course not.

Sister   You are. You're scared of everything you. You are entirely defined by your fear.

Brother   It's not about fear it's about medical and legal responsibility. I'm not scared in any way.

Sister   Show me then. Show me you're not scared.

Are you getting a hard-on?

Brother   A bit of one.

Sister   Is that to show me how unafraid you are?

Brother   I don't think hard-ons are as conscious as that.

Sister   That's shocking that is.

Brother   I'm fourteen years old, I nearly always have a hard-on.

Sister   You're so cute.

I might snog you.

Brother   Don't.

Sister   Why not? Are you scared about that as well? We wouldn't need to tell anybody.

Brother   People would find out.

Sister   Wouldn't need to tell Mum and Dad.

Brother   I can't.

Sister   You can.

It's New Year. Nobody would know. A whole new start to a whole new world. Who knows what's going to happen tonight? Everything is being turned upside down. For one night only we can do anything. We can go anywhere. I can stick my tongue down your throat and nobody would mind. I could bite your ears off. Chew into the ligament. Make sure they come off. Keep chewing. Nobody need ever know. Nobody need ever know anything.

*

Passenger   I was just drinking.

Redhead Boy   You were doing more than that.

Passenger   I was just trying to get off my head.

Redhead Boy   You were all over him.

Passenger   I was trying to forget everything that happened.

Redhead Boy   You stuck your tongue down his throat.

Passenger   I wanted to remember what it felt like to kiss a boy.

Redhead Boy   You practically had his cock down your throat.

Passenger   I'd forgotten. It had been so long.

Redhead Boy   You had his cock in your ear.

Passenger   I was trying to forget the shape of words.

Redhead Boy   You had his head up your skirt.

Passenger   I was trying to forget what the world looked like.

Redhead Boy   You had your face up his arse.

Passenger   I was looking for my fucking soul. I thought I must have left it somewhere.

Redhead Boy   You had your shoe up his balls.

Passenger   At least he fucking had balls. At least he had a heart. At least he had an arse. At least there was somewhere for me to go.

*

Ralph Lauren   Do you love me?

Girl Who Sparkles   Yes I love you.

Ralph Lauren   You're just saying that.

Girl Who Sparkles   I'm not. I love you.

Ralph Lauren   You don't know me.

Girl Who Sparkles   I know you *so* well.

Ralph Lauren   You met me an hour ago.

Girl Who Sparkles   It's magical isn't it?

Ralph Lauren   You don't even know my name.

Girl Who Sparkles   I don't need to know your name. I know what you taste like. I know how your skin feels. I know the feeling of your shirt. I know the feeling of your stupid fucking dick of a tie. And the feeling of your hand on my arse. And the taste of chips and burger and chewing gum in your mouth.

Ralph Lauren   Will you stay with me?

Girl Who Sparkles   Until the actual end of time.

Ralph Lauren   It's nearly the start of a whole new year.

Girl Who Sparkles   It's exciting isn't it?

Ralph Lauren   Are you drunk?

Girl Who Sparkles   No. No. No. No. No. No. No. A bit. Not really. No. Yes. Very.

Ralph Lauren   Don't lie to me about things like that.

Girl Who Sparkles   I'm not lying.

Ralph Lauren   I swear please. I don't want you to lie to me about that or about anything.

Girl Who Sparkles   I won't.

Ralph Lauren   Everybody lies to me. If somebody lies to me one more time I don't know what I'll do.

Girl Who Sparkles   Baby.

Ralph Lauren   Don't call me baby. I'm not your baby.

Girl Who Sparkles   Shhh. It was meant to be nice. I was trying to be nice.

Ralph Lauren   Are you cold?

Girl Who Sparkles   No.

Ralph Lauren   Do you want to borrow my jacket?

Girl Who Sparkles   I'm not cold.

Ralph Lauren   I like your hat.

Girl Who Sparkles   Thank you.

Ralph Lauren   And your dress. The way it shimmers.

Girl Who Sparkles   It doesn't shimmer. It sparkles.

Ralph Lauren   You are about the most beautiful girl I've
ever seen in my life and I want to lend you my jacket and
look after you always and hold your hand when the New Year
starts and always be with you and fight to save your life and
fight to save your country and go off to war and come back
injured and you can look after me and feed me soup and kiss
my wounds and take photos of me when I'm not looking and
always be there and always be smiling when the New Year
counts down I want you always to be smiling.

Girl Who Sparkles   I want that too.

Ralph Lauren   Do you?

Girl Who Sparkles   I do. I swear. I do. I really do.

*

Grinning Boy   It's the booze.

Redhead Boy   It's not the booze. I've not even drunk that
much.

Grinning Boy   You have.

Redhead Boy   I've not.

Grinning Boy   You've been drinking since three o'clock.
Eaten shit all day.

Redhead Boy It's not the food either. I've not eaten anything.

Grinning Boy Have you been smoking?

Redhead Boy Not skunk. Just a bit of weed. Nothing serious.

Grinning Boy You finished yet?

Redhead Boy I don't know.

Grinning Boy I can't stand here all night.

Redhead Boy I just feel –

Grinning Boy What?

Redhead Boy There's just something I need to get out.

Grinning Boy Get out? Of like your stomach?

Redhead Boy Of my body.

Grinning Boy Are you cold?

Redhead Boy Am I fuck cold?

Grinning Boy You're shivering.

Redhead Boy That's not cos I'm cold.

Grinning Boy Why you fucking shivering then?

Redhead Boy I don't know.

Grinning Boy What do you mean you don't know?

Redhead Boy I wasn't even aware that I was shivering. Can you hear that?

Grinning Boy Hear what?

Redhead Boy That sound?

Grinning Boy What sound? There are sounds all over the place.

Redhead Boy   Like singing?

Grinning Boy   Probably fucking 'Auld Lang Syne' at this rate. People singing for the New Year.

Redhead Boy   What time is it?

Grinning Boy   I have no fucking idea.

Redhead Boy   Is it the New Year yet?

Grinning Boy   I don't think so. No. You'd have heard. There'd have been like car horns and shit.

Redhead Boy   It's like angels.

But like dark angels. Dark. Fuck.

Grinning Boy   What are you going on about?

Redhead Boy   Mate.

Grinning Boy   Yes.

Redhead Boy   Mate.

Grinning Boy   Yes.

Redhead Boy   Am I standing on the ground?

Grinning Boy   What do you mean?

Redhead Boy   My feet, are they on the ground?

Grinning Boy   Have you had some pills?

Redhead Boy   You know I haven't. I've not done pills for fucking, for – It's not pills. I just feel. So. Sad.

Grinning Boy   Is this about Sarah?

Redhead Boy   No.

Grinning Boy   Is it about Charlotte?

Redhead Boy   No. Maybe. No.

Grinning Boy   Is it about your dad?

Redhead Boy   Maybe. It might be. It might be about him.

Am I gonna be all right?

Grinning Boy   What the fuck is that supposed to mean? 'Am I gonna be all right?' What kind of a fucking question is that man? Fuckssake. 'Am I gonna be all right?' I don't know, do I? How am I meant to know about something like that?

Redhead Boy   Sorry.

Grinning Boy   Fucking weirdo.

What are you sad about?

Redhead Boy   I have this sense that something's going to happen.

Grinning Boy   Something is gonna happen, mate. I'm gonna fucking fuck off. Leave you here on your own. Come and get you in the morning.

Redhead Boy   Not like that.

Grinning Boy   Like what then?

Redhead Boy   Something worse than that. Something fucking horrible. Something – Something –

*

Grinning Boy   I'm not scared.

Don't look at me like I'm scared because I'm not fucking scared.

I'm not scared of what's going to happen, I'm not scared of the noises.

It's raining. It's water. There's nothing frightening about rain. And when the New Year comes, and everything changes, then, you'll see.

I will dance with a lightness you have never before seen on any other human being. I will be as free as a bird. I will be as light as a skylark. I will show you things you never thought you'd see. I will take you places you never thought you'd go.

And the noises, the noises, those noises. The noises will stop.

*

Police 1   Calm down.

Passenger   Get off me.

Police 2   Mind her head.

Passenger   Get off me I said.

Police 1   I'm going to ask you one more time to calm down, Miss, and come with us.

Brother   You seen the state of her?

Police 3   Can we get these two out of here?

Sister   You can't move us.

Police 3   Sorry, sweetheart, I need you to move away from here.

Sister   Don't call me sweetheart. I'm not your sweetheart. I'm filming this.

Brother   Police brutality that is.

Police 3   Right. Great. Smashing.

Passenger   You're hurting me.

Police 1   We're not trying to hurt you.

Police 2   I hate this.

Police 4   What?

Police 2   I'm tired of this.

Police 4   New Year's Eve, Michael, it's what happens, pal.

Police 2   It's nothing to do with the New Year.

Police 3   Careful with the arm, chaps.

Police 1   I'm being careful.

Passenger   I'm calling the telly on you.

Police 1   You're calling who?

Passenger   The telly. I'm gonna get you on telly. You are going to be so fucked.

Police 1   Please calm down.

Passenger   You are going to be fucked. They are going to have your badge. They are going to have your job. I'm going to have your job.

Brother   This is hilarious.

Sister   I am totally going to piss myself.

Police 1   Young lady I'm giving you one last opportunity to come quietly with me.

Driver   Get her out of my fucking cab.

Police 2   Sir, please. There is no need to use language like that.

Driver   Yes there fucking is. Of course there fucking is. She puked in my taxi. I've got to clean that now. She pissed in my taxi. It fucking stinks.

Police 4   That's why we're here, sir.

Police 2   We're trying to help you.

Passenger   You're hurting me.

Police 1   Young lady. Please stop trying to resist.

Passenger   How long is it now? Until the New Year?

Police 2   An hour. Just under.

Passenger   I'm calling my dad.

Police 1   You can do that as soon as you leave this gentleman's car.

Passenger   He's not a gentleman. Don't call him a gentleman. He's not a gentleman. He's a fucking Paki. He's a fucking nigger. He's a fucking Al Quaeda he is. He's a raghead fucking ISIS cunt.

Police 3   Miss, I'm going to ask you to refrain from using language like that.

Brother   Classic.

Passenger   I'm gonna have him.

Police 1   I'm sure you are.

Sister   Seven shares and seventeen likes already. Epic.

Passenger   Should have heard the things he was saying.

Sister   You should read the things people are saying in the comments about you, love.

Passenger   Don't call me love. I'm not your fucking love.

Driver   I wasn't saying anything.

Passenger   Saying how he's gonna bomb us.

Police 4   Lovely.

Passenger   Gonna nail bomb us. Gonna put fucking poison in our drinks. Gonna rip our eyes out. That's what he said.

Driver   I never.

Passenger   You did right. You fucking Paki lying ISIS cunt.

Driver   I never said anything like that.

Police 2   I'm going to ask you one more time.

Passenger   Gonna hang me out of his flat window. Gonna drag me along chained to the boot of his car.

Police 2   Please stop talking now.

Passenger   Gonna cut my biceps with his garden shears. Gonna marry me even though I don't want to. Gonna come over here. Gonna come over here. To my country.

Police 2   I'm being polite.

Passenger   Gonna take over my country and make me wear a burka and make me drink battery acid and get his cock out and have a wank and shit the bed and whack it on Snapchat and sing for queen and country and never never never go home any more.

Police 2   Please stop.

*

Driver   I wonder what she's called. Hey. You. Hey. What's your name?

Aren't you going to tell me? Won't they let you tell me?

I wonder where her dad is. Hey. Sweetheart. Where's your dad? Where's your father? Does he know you're out tonight? Does he know what state you're in? Would you like me to tell him? You give me his number and I'll call him? What's your dad's phone number? Officer. Can you ask her to tell me her dad's phone number?

Does he know where you are?

They're hurting her. Don't hurt her. She's only a child. She's a child.

If she were my daughter I wouldn't let her come out like this.

Is she laughing? Are you laughing? Stop laughing. You stupid –
stupid – stupid – stupid –

That's my car now. That smell. That smell of sick and vodka.
That will be in my car for days and no matter how much I
clean it I won't be able to clean it out. It will be in my nose
for days and no matter what I taste or drink or how much
I clean I won't be able to get rid of it. Once you've seen
something like that you can never get rid of it. Once you've
smelt something like that you can never get rid of it.

I'll give it one more hour. At most. Then go home and make
sure my wife's all right.

Four more fares. At most. Maybe it's not too late to get an
airport run. Maybe I can get an airport run even now. Some
rich couple. Drive them out to the airport. Maybe somebody
needs to go to another city. Maybe not everybody will be
drunk.

What are they doing to her? These police. Officer. Officer,
can I go yet? Officer, what are you doing? Is he crying? Is
that policeman crying? Officer, are you crying? Are they
tears? Officer, are they tears?

*

Passenger   Do you know any songs?

Police 1   Young lady, can you move away from the road
now please?

Passenger   Do you ever get like you just want to sing
songs?

Police 1   The more you resist the more painful it will be.

Police 2   Is there a member of your family we could
contact?

Passenger   No. There are no members of my family. My family are all dead.

Police 1   Is there anybody you'd like us to contact regarding your arrest tonight?

Passenger   They were all killed in acts of police brutality! They weren't really. They're not even dead. They just don't like me. Are you arresting me?

Police 1   Did you not hear what we said to you earlier?

Passenger   You have the right to remain silent but blah blah blah blah blah. I've got a great singing voice, me.

Police 1   I'm sure you have.

Passenger   I haven't sung for ages.

Police 1   I'm sure you've not.

Police 2   I haven't either.

I haven't.

I used to sing.

Police 3   Did you?

Police 2   I was in the church choir.

Police 3   I didn't know you went to church.

Police 2   I don't any more. I did when I was younger. I stayed in the church for years afterwards largely on account of the singing.

Passenger   I'll sing with you.

Police 2   It's very rare nowadays to get the opportunity to do communal singing.

Police 1   We need to get you into the van.

Passenger   You don't.

Police 2 I would cherish it. It's just I lost all faith in the idea of a life after death and I came to find the superstition of it all unbearable.

Police 1 Young lady, we're going to take you to the station where we're going to charge you.

Passenger What for?

Police 1 For the racially aggravated assault of a police officer and vandalism of a taxi cab.

Passenger I never touched anybody.

Police 4 We could sing 'Auld Lang Syne'.

Passenger You can't charge me.

Police 1 If you just raise your right elbow a little.

Police 4 I love 'Auld Lang Syne', me.

Police 2 I do too. I love the poetry of Robbie Burns on the whole. It has a surface simplicity that belies a depth of sadness and rage that many of his peers in England lacked.

Passenger If you charge me I'll definitely go down.

Police 2 I like sad poems. I like sad things on the whole. I find them uplifting in the end. Far more uplifting than art that is intended to inspire or galvanise people or cheer them up. Which is odd. Because I'm not a downbeat person on the whole. I'm a jolly soul. I'm a cheerful little sprite. I'm very sorry to hear about your family. It's always dislocating when our families turn against us.

Police 1 If you don't raise your right arm it could cause you quite acute pain.

Passenger I've done this before. I'm on a warning.

Police 1 I'm sure you are. You broke a police officer's nose. And called him a 'fat fucking nig-nog'.

Passenger I never.

Police 2   You did. I'm afraid.

Passenger   Please don't. Please don't. Please don't. Please don't.

Police 1   Young lady, please calm down.

Passenger (*singing*)   'Should auld acquaintance be forgot' –

Police 2 *and* **Passenger**   'And never come to rise' –

Police 4   Classic.

Police 1   Young lady –

Passenger   'We'll drink a glass of kindness yet' –

Police 4   Is he alright? Our reputable colleague? Has he gone to hospital?

Police 3   A while ago.

Police 1   A fucking shit night for the hospital tonight.

Police 3   They'll see him as quick as they can.

Police 4   Put a paper hat on his head. Sit him in A&E with a bottle of brandy.

Passenger   'For the sake of Auld Lang Syne.'

Police 1   Thank you, young lady. Are you alright? Have you calmed down now? Are you calm?

*

Girl With No Shoes   You're going to fall.

Girl With Trainers   I'm not.

Girl With No Shoes   You'll break your neck.

Girl With Trainers   I'm never going to fall me.

Girl With No Shoes   You'll break your phone.

Girl With Trainers   No way. I have an unconquerable steel grip on my phone.

Girl With No Shoes   You'll look a right dick.

Girl With Trainers   I will not look a dick. I will never look anything other than gracious.

Girl With No Shoes   Gracious? What kind of word is 'gracious'?

Girl With Trainers   It is a fucking accurate word. It describes with fucking accuracy exactly how I am going to look.

Woman Who Can See Under The World   She's funny.

Girl With No Shoes   She's stupid.

Woman Who Can See Under The World   I like her.

Girl With No Shoes   You would.

Girl With Trainers   Not just tonight.

Girl With No Shoes   What do you mean not just tonight?

Girl With Trainers   For the whole of next year.

Woman Who Can See Under The World   That couple are watching you. I think she's taking taking a photo of you.

Girl With Trainers   I don't blame her. She's right to take a photo of me. She should make a film of me. She should make a documentary about me. She should make a fucking concept album about me.

Woman Who Can See Under The World   Petal.

Girl With Trainers   She should build statues of me. She should write operas about me. This year people are going to write operas about me. And build buildings inspired by me. This whole next year I am going to pass my exams. I am going to leave this city. I am going to leave this country. I am going to never come home.

Woman Who Can See Under The World   You better had.

Girl With No Shoes   She will.

Woman Who Can See Under The World   She better.

Girl With Trainers   I am going to make my debut as a professional footballer.

Girl With No Shoes   You're shit at football.

Girl With Trainers   And build my first skyscraper. And win a Michelin star.

Girl With No Shoes   You can't cook.

Girl With Trainers   I will this year. I am going to learn to cook. And learn to speak three new languages. And learn to fly a plane. And work out. And get a six-pack.

Girl With No Shoes   You are not going to get a six-pack.

Girl With Trainers   And run a hundred metres in less than nine seconds. And cross the Sahara on a motorbike. And cross the Sahara on a bicycle. And cross the Sahara in a speedboat. And lift ten tonnes of steel in the fist of one hand and sing opera with the voice of an angel and rap with more rhyming complexity and intellectual incision than anybody thought possible and dance with Uma Thurman and dance with John Travolta and dance with Gene Kelly.

Girl With No Shoes   All three of those people are definitely dead.

Girl With Trainers   And direct the next *Star Wars* film. And make an album with Kendrick Lamar and make a baby with Taylor Swift.

Woman Who Can See Under The World   Taylor Swift?

Girl With Trainers   And marry you.

Girl With No Shoes   You what?

Girl With Trainers   This year I am going to marry you.

Girl With No Shoes   Fuck off.

Girl With Trainers   It's true.

Girl With No Shoes   You're being daft.

Woman Who Can See Under The World   She is.

Girl With No Shoes   I know she is.

Girl With Trainers   I'm not.

Woman Who Can See Under The World   Don't.

Pause.

It's nearly midnight.

Girl With Trainers   I know it's nearly midnight.

Woman Who Can See Under The World   We should get going. We don't want to miss the Countdown.

Girl With Trainers   Stay there.

Girl With No Shoes   Will you come down for fuck's sake?

Girl With Trainers   This year.

Girl With No Shoes   You're so buzzing.

Girl With Trainers   I'm not.

Woman Who Can See Under The World   She's off her face.

Girl With Trainers   Will you marry me?

Girl With No Shoes   No.

Girl With Trainers   Please. I'm being serious.

Woman Who Can See Under The World   Don't do this.

Girl With Trainers   I am being more serious than I have ever been before.

Woman Who Can See Under The World   I'm going.

Girl With Trainers   Please. Will you marry me? This year? Will you?

*

Woman Who Can See Under The World   Shhh.

Stay extremely still.

Come here.

Slowly. No. More slowly than that. Don't make any sudden noises. Here. Come here. Look here. Look. Down here.

Can you see?

Down here. In the corner of the wall. There's a hole.

Can you see it? Can you see the hole?

Can you see what's down there?

I'm not sure, but I think. I think. I think it's the bottom of the world.

Can you see the people down there? There's so many of them. They must be able to see me. I must look enormous to them. Like an enormous eye staring down a crack in the ceiling. I think they're dancing with each other. And smiling. I can't see a single one of them fighting. Or hurting one another. Or screaming. I can't hear any of them screaming. I think they're drinking water. I think some of them might be ice-skating. I think they're kissing.

And there are birds down there. And I can see other mammals too. Zebras and giraffes and horses. There are hundreds of tiny horses under the surface of the world.

Don't tell anybody.

And the colours down there are so bright. It's quiet. Can you hear how quiet it is?

My dad's down there. Hi Dad. And my grandmother. And little baby Jason's down there. Is that the Queen? No. She can't be? Does anybody know? Has the Queen died? No.

Dad?

Grandma?

I've not been drinking anything. I've got a tiny bird in my hand. I have to hold it gently between my fingers. You mustn't drink when you have a position of responsibility like that. You mustn't. You can't.

Four **Policemen** *hold the* **Redhead Boy** *tightly with his arms behind his back. As the scene goes on the boy screams and screams and screams.*

Police 3   What time are you finishing, Michael?

Police 2   Three o'clock.

Police 3   The last two hours. That's always the hardest bit.

Police 1   I'm starving as well.

Police 3   We could go to McDonald's.

Police 4   I fucking hate McDonald's.

Police 3   Easy though.

Police 1   Call back to the base, get them to call us an Indian.

Police 3   What do you fancy?

Police 4   A chicken pasanda.

Police 1   Nice.

Police 3   Just get a selection. Get a few. We can split the cost.

The **Redhead Boy** *screams louder.*

Police 2   Is he breathing?

Police 4   Course he's breathing.

Police 2   How long has he been screaming now?

Police 1   Fucking ages.

Police 4   Five minutes.

Police 2   Five minutes without taking a breath.

Police 1   Is it me or does he smell funny?

Police 3   He does smell a bit peculiar.

Police 1   What is that smell?

Police 4   Is it blood?

Police 2   Have you cut yourself, son?

Police 1   Are you bleeding?

Police 4   If he's bleeding that will be a right pain.

Police 1   We'll have to get checked up. Blood checks. All that. The fucking paperwork.

Police 4   Oy. Son. Stop screaming. Stop it. Stop crying. Hey. Dickhead. Can you hear me? Shut the fuck up?

Police 3   I always enjoy the charged sense of anticipation of any given New Year's Eve.

Police 4   Festive, isn't it?

Police 3   You got any resolutions?

Police 1   I'm going to smoke more cigarettes.

Police 4   Nice one.

Police 1   Drink more booze.

Police 2   I'm going to read a novel every week.

Police 4   Are you?

Police 1   That's impressive, that is.

Police 2   And listen to albums. Instead of playing music on like shuffle and that. I'm going to listen to more albums.

Police 1   On vinyl.

Police 2   Not necessarily vinyl now, I just want to consider the whole experience of an album rather than taking tracks randomly in different orders.

Did you hear that?

Police 1   What?

Police 2   I thought I heard a cracking sound.

Police 1   Fuck off.

Police 3   Did you?

Police 4   In his arm?

Police 3   Hey lad? Are you all right?

Police 4   Did they break your arm?

Police 3   I don't think 'they' is the right pronoun there, mate. It was nothing to do with me.

Police 4   Yeah, that was definitely your fault.

Police 1   No it wasn't.

Police 4   You are so done. Racially provoked police brutality. The paperwork on you, mate.

Police 1   How's that racially provoked?

Police 4   White boy innit?

Police 1   Oh do fuck off.

Police 4   Aggressive police officer picking on the white boys. On New Year's Eve.

Police 1   Fuck off. I said.

Fucking hell.

Police 3   She's teasing.

Police 1   I know.

It's cos her back is giving her stress. Her lumber.

Police 2   You should get it checked out.

Police 4   I know.

Police 2   Go to an osteopath.

Police 4   I know.

Police 2   I do Pilates.

Police 1   Do you?

Police 2   That sorts me out, no problem. I'll give you a number. Make that your resolution.

Police 1   Less porn and more Pilates.

Police 3   Well. I don't think resolutions need to be so prohibitive.

Police 1   Less Japanese porn and more Pilates.

Police 4   Yeah. Alright.

Police 1   Less porn in a language that you can't understand with boys who are definitely young enough to be your son and more Pilates.

Police 3   New Year's resolutions can be as positive as they are negative.

Police 2   Has he stopped?

Police 1   Has he?

Police 2   Has he stopped screaming?

Police 1   He has.

Police 3   He's all right.

Police 1   He has. You have.

Police 2   He's asleep.

Police 1   Hey. Hey sunshine. Hey sunshine, hey. Wake up.

*

Sister   And hold it and freeze. And there!

Police 1   Hold on.

Police 2   Can we go again?

Police 1   My hat wasn't right.

Police 2   It looks fine.

Police 1   Just give us a sec.

Police 3   Can I say something?

Police 1   I have a feeling you're going to.

Police 3   I don't think he's giving us enough.

Police 1   Mate. Mate. What's your name? Do you think you could give us a little bit more?

Redhead Boy   More what?

Police 1   More anger?

Police 3   Is it anger?

Police 2   I'm not sure anger is the right word.

Police 3   More dislocation?

Police 2   Can you give us more dislocation?

Police 1   Try to think of something that dislocates you.

Redhead Boy   I don't even know what that means.

Police 4   No.

Police 3   Like. When you think about the world. And there is a difference between the way the world is and the way you want the world to be.

Police 4   In your head.

Redhead Boy   Right.

Police 3   You know what I mean?

Redhead Boy   I think so.

Like I can't get the right pen?

Police 3   What do you mean?

Redhead Boy   There are like pens that I want. And I can't find them. I have this idea of what the pen should be and how it should write and no matter what I do or where I look I can't find it.

Police 4   Pens?

Redhead Boy   Yeah.

Police 4   Seriously?

Police 3   That kind of thing.

Police 4   Pens?

Police 1   Think about your pen.

Police 4   Is that the best you can do?

Police 3   If you think that will help.

Redhead Boy   I think it might.

Police 3   Great.

Police 1   Smashing.

Redhead Boy   Or sometimes, yes?

Police 4   What?

Redhead Boy   In a restaurant. There are people singing.

Police 4   What do you mean?

Redhead Boy   I went to a restaurant and there were these people in there singing. They were singing 'American Pie' by Don McLean and it was embarrassing because the other people in the restaurant wanted to just have their meals.

Police 4   Fucking hell.

Police 3   That's the ticket. Think about that.

Redhead Boy   And it wasn't as though it was a posh restaurant.

Police 3   I'm sure it wasn't.

Redhead Boy   It was a normal restaurant. But these people. They were like fucking rich and fucking posh and like some of them were American but not all of them and I just wanted to go up to their table and tip it up and smash their plates in their faces and their cutlery in their eyes and look at them and say 'No. This is not what people should do to other people in public places. That is just not fair. Fuck you. Fuck you. Fuck you. Fuck you.'

Police 4   That's great.

Police 3   Use that.

Police 4   Channel it.

Police 1   Yes.

Police 3   Channel that.

Police 1   But maybe something more particular too.

Redhead Boy   Like the pen?

Police 1   Yes. The combination of the Americans in the restaurant and your missing pen would be just perfect.

Redhead Boy   And Jews.

Police 2   What?

Redhead Boy   The way Jewish people smell.

Police 2   What?

Redhead Boy   That makes me angry as well.

Police 2   What?

Redhead Boy   I get really angry when I think about the way Jewish people smell and I think I'd like to channel that.

Police 1   That's a bit rude.

Police 3   I think very rude.

Police 1   A bit anti-semitic.

Police 4   A bit racist.

Police 2   Fucking racist actually.

Police 1   Are you a bit racist?

Redhead Boy   No. I just want the photo to look right.

Police 4   We want that too.

Police 1   That's very important to us.

Police 4   Think about those things if you think it will help.

Redhead Boy   I am.

Police 1   Good lad.

Redhead Boy   Really hard.

Police 3   Racism in any form is inexcusable.

Police 1   How's my hat?

Police 2   It's straight.

Police 4   And count down from three.

Sister   Three. Two. One.

*

Woman In A Flowery Dress   I just got nervous.

Driver   I know you did.

Woman In A Flowery Dress   I won't be able to sleep now.

Driver   Don't be silly.

Woman In A Flowery Dress   I'm not being silly. You know what I'm like.

Driver   Hey.

Woman In A Flowery Dress   I'll have nightmares.

Driver   Come on.

Woman In A Flowery Dress   It's the way they look at you.

Driver   They're harmless.

Woman In A Flowery Dress   And the noises they make.

Driver   They're just barking.

Woman In A Flowery Dress   And the way they move.

Driver   You're being silly.

Woman In A Flowery Dress   And they smell. They smell horrible. And it's the same smell. I recognise it. I only need to walk into the room where they've been. And they bite. People say they don't bite or they don't all bite only if you make them angry or you corner them but they do bite. I've seen them, I know it.

Driver   You're being irrational.

Woman In A Flowery Dress   I know I'm being irrational. I know that, darling. But it's an irrational fear. The whole point of an irrational fear is that it is irrational. I'm sorry.

Driver   You don't need to be sorry. Just do your breathing.

Woman In A Flowery Dress   Okay.

Driver   In. 1, 2, 3, 4, 5, 6, 7, 8, 9, 10. Out. 1, 2, 3, 4, 5, 6, 7, 8, 9, 10.

Woman In A Flowery Dress   Thank you.

Driver   That's all right.

Woman In A Flowery Dress   I don't know what I'd do without you.

Driver   You'd be fine.

Woman In A Flowery Dress   I would so not be fine. I'd be lying there. In the street. Unable to move.

Driver   But I am here.

Woman In A Flowery Dress   What are they doing here, darling?

Driver   They're harmless.

Woman In A Flowery Dress   This is my street.

Driver   I know.

Woman In A Flowery Dress   They shouldn't be allowed in my street.

Driver   Shhh.

Woman In A Flowery Dress   People are just careless. That's the problem. They don't think. They don't think about what's going to happen. They don't think about other people. They don't think about the future. They try to be so nice and calm but they're not thinking about how dangerous these people are. I don't know what they want or what they're going to do and what they're going to do to me.

Driver   They're not going to do anything to you.

Woman In A Flowery Dress   They are though.

Why's he singing?

Driver   I think it must have started.

Woman In A Flowery Dress   What must have started?

Driver   The New Year.

Woman In A Flowery Dress   Has it?

Driver   I think so.

Woman In A Flowery Dress   That's nice.

Driver   Hey. Hey. Hey mate? Is this it? Is this the New year? Has it started now?

*

Woman With A Bag   It's not enough to say it's over

Man With Sideburns   It is.

Woman With A Bag   You haven't even got a clue what that means.

Man With Sideburns   Calm down.

Woman With A Bag   Don't fucking tell me to calm down. You don't know what you're talking about, calm down. This is important. This matters.

Man With Sideburns   I know it matters.

Woman With A Bag   This is about everything.

Man With Sideburns   I know.

Woman With A Bag   Nothing else is important if we let this go.

Man With Sideburns   Nobody's letting it go.

Woman With A Bag   Nothing matters if we just give up on it.

Man With Sideburns   Please. People are looking.

Woman With A Bag   I don't care if people are looking. I don't care if the world is looking. I don't care about any of that. I don't care about what people think. Here. On this street. In this city. If we let this end then everything ends. This whole street ends if we stop this.

Man With Sideburns   I don't want to do it any more.

Woman With A Bag   You have to.

Man With Sideburns   I don't.

Woman With A Bag   Money doesn't matter. Words don't matter. Our bodies don't matter. Stories don't matter. Our colour doesn't matter, our clothes don't matter. Our skin doesn't matter. Nothing matters. All we've got is this simple idea and it's an idea you can't walk away from.

Man With Sideburns   I can.

Brother   He can.

Woman With A Bag   Shut the fuck up, you stupid fucking total cunt you have no fucking idea what the fuck I am talking about.

Brother   Jesus, sweetheart.

Woman With A Bag   Don't you sweetheart me.

Sister   You're spitting now. That's horrible.

Woman With A Bag   That is not horrible. I'll tell you what's horrible. This is horrible. The idea that we can walk away from this is horrible. Everything that ever meant anything to anybody ends if you turn and walk away. The borders come down. The bombs fly upwards sucked into planes in the sky. The grass sinks into the earth. The animals shrink and climb into their mothers' wombs. Words go backwards and end up like sad strange sucking sounds. People walk backwards onto trains. Countries dissolve. Spreadsheets dissolve. Light shows dissolve. Literature dissolves. There is such a thing as humanity and it ends now. If you walk away from this.

Man With Sideburns   That's not how it works.

Woman With A Bag   It is. It is. It so fucking is. Please tell me you understand that it is because it is.

I love you.

Man With Sideburns   I know that.

Woman With A Bag   I hate myself for loving you but I love you.

Man With Sideburns   I know.

Woman With A Bag   If you turn and walk away from this it won't be an easy thing.

Man With Sideburns   I know.

Woman With A Bag   For either of us.

Man With Sideburns   No.

Woman With A Bag   So don't.

Man With Sideburns   I have to.

Woman With A Bag   Don't.

Man With Sideburns   I want to.

Woman With A Bag   Don't.

*

Helicopter Boy   What the fuck do you think you're doing?

You fucking blind bastards.

What the fuck did you say, you fucking screw-headed little fucking piggyback fascist shites?

Right. That is it. I will cut your faces off.

Are you telling me what to say?

Are you actually correcting me, you fascist fucks?

Stay fucking there. If you move one more muscle I will lacerate you.

I will slice your skin into bits and make a chain of your fingernails.

I will play your fucking lungs like my fucking bagpipes.

Do you think I won't?

Do you think I daren't?

Do you think I can't?

Brother   He does a lot of talking, doesn't he? But if you watch he's not actually done anything.

Helicopter Boy   As from tonight. As from this moment. We have had enough. We are done. You can't stop us any more.

We have had enough of your shortcuts and your measures taken. We have had enough of the promises you broke and the way you sniggered up your sleeves. From this point we take everything back. From this point we requisition your property. We take ownership of the means of production. We forcibly redistribute your stolen wealth. You can't hold us back any more.

Sister   He's just stood there in the middle of road waving his arms around like a helicopter and coming up with a series of increasingly unlikely threats.

Helicopter Boy   We will turn you into an effigy and dance on your spoilt millionaire children's faces with our fucking bare feet.

Are you laughing at me?

I am going to have the world you made for yourselves and protected for yourselves and I am going to get it and I am going to share that fucker out.

Can you hear that noise? That's the sound of us coming to take back what is owed to us. That's the sound of this country changing. That's the sound of your world falling the fuck apart.

Crowd   10, 9, 8, 7, 6, 5, 4, 3, 2, 1! Happy New Year!

The crowd sing 'Auld Lang Syne'.

*

Police 1   Get him.

Police 4   Get his jaw.

Police 1   Get his knees.

Police 4   Crack his kneecaps.

Helicopter Boy   No please.

Police 1   Shut up. Now.

Helicopter Boy   I'm sorry.

Police 1   Bit late for that, son.

Police 4   Get his right arm.

Police 1   Break his fingers.

Police 4   Break his arm.

Helicopter Boy   No. Don't. Please. Don't. Please don't hurt me.

Police 1   Get his jaw.

Police 4   Break his jaw.

Girl With No Shoes   Officer?

Police 1   Don't 'Officer' me or I swear to all things wonderful you will be the next to take the fall.

Police 4   Smash his thigh bones.

Police 1   Brace his neck.

Police 4   Stranglehold.

Police 1   Put your foot on his windpipe.

Police 4   Press down.

Helicopter Boy   Please no.

Police 4   Harder.

Press harder.

Jump. Jump on his neck.

This boy is resisting arrest.

Girl With No Shoes   That boy is not resisting arrest.

Police 4   Listen, Kunta Kinte, if you don't keep your fat lips sealed tight I will come over there and cut the fuckers off and keep them as a memento in the wallet where I keep my fucking ID card.

Girl With No Shoes   He's crying.

Police 4   I know he's crying. He's a toerag.

Police 1   He's not worth your concern.

Police 4   He's an illegal immigrant.

Police 1   He's from the suburbs of Bucharest. He's homophobic and violent. He's involved in ketamine import and child pornography.

Girl With No Shoes   That's not true.

Police 1   We're taking him in.

Girl With No Shoes   You don't need to stand on his neck.

Police 1   It was a conventional brace hold. He was resisting arrest.

Girl With No Shoes   He wasn't.

Police 4   Do you want me to demonstrate?

Girl With No Shoes   No.

Police 4   Do you want me to show you what it's like to fucking resist arrest?

Girl With No Shoes   No.

Police 4   Because I will.

Girl With No Shoes   No.

Is he breathing?

Police 4   That's none of your concern.

Girl With No Shoes   It doesn't look like he's breathing.

Police 1   Miss. Miss. Miss. Please will you go back inside, please, Miss?

Girl Who Sparkles   Be careful.

Police 2   Madam, thank you. Please move to the side.

Girl Who Sparkles   He's epileptic.

Police 1   You have the right to remain silent.

Helicopter Boy   I need to get my pen. I need my epipen. I'm flipping out.

Man In Blue   I can just. Reach. It.

Police 2   Madam, I'm going to ask you again one more time.

Police 1   Sir, if you resist it will hurt a lot more. Try to relax.

Police 2   Have you seen the blood on his face?

Helicopter Boy   Am I bleeding? I can't do bleeding. Please God.

Man In Blue   I'm all right. I'm all right. You don't need to worry. I'm all right.

Police 4   Is he your boyfriend, Madam?

Girl Who Sparkles   No. He's not my boyfriend. I just know him. Everybody round here knows him. Everybody knows him.

Girl With No Shoes   We were leaving the nightclub and he was there and his arms were flapping around and it was like he was kind of screaming but he didn't actually do anything but his arms kept going round and round like a like a like a like a like a —

Brother   Is that policeman crying?

Sister   They are so dead.

Brother   That's police brutality.

Man In Blue   It's the night-time. And I am asleep. I am asleep in the night-time and if I just reach one more stretch further then it will be the daytime and I will wake all over again and everything will be fine.

Girl With No Shoes   He didn't hurt anybody.

Police 3   Was he resisting arrest?

Girl With No Shoes   No.

Police 2   Please sir. Relax your arm.

Police 3   Would you say that his resistance was particularly aggressive to all of the officers or one in particular?

Girl With No Shoes   He wasn't resisting arrest.

Helicopter Boy   I need my fucking pen. I'm having an allergic shock.

Police 1   What are you allergic to, sir?

Helicopter Boy   I'm not allergic. I'm epileptic.

Girl Who Sparkles   You should get a Biro. You're gonna need to put a Biro in his throat. He won't be able to breathe.

Girl With No Shoes   It was like he was a helicopter.
Flapping your arms round like a helicopter is not the same
as resisting arrest.

Brother   Hashtag policebrutality.

Sister   That one's cute.

Brother   Which one?

Sister   The one holding his wrists back.

Man In Blue   This is just like school. It's just like playing
games at school. All I need to do is concentrate.

Girl With No Shoes   I like the police.

Police 2   That's good to hear.

Girl With No Shoes   I like the police round here
especially.

Police 2   I'm very glad about that, Madam.

Girl With No Shoes   But that is just wrong.

Police 2   What is just wrong?

Girl With No Shoes   He never hurt anybody.

Police 3   We have got CCTV coverage that will definitely
point to the idea that what he was doing was resisting arrest.

Brother   Hey. Hey. Hey. Look.

Have you seen him? He's gonna reach it. Do you think he's
going to reach his beer? I do. I think he will. I like him. I
think he's all right. I think he's amazing. Hey. Mister. Mister.
Mister. Mister. I think you're amazing.

Woman With A Tiara   If you kill him I swear I will tell
everybody I saw you.

Police 2   Miss. Please. You're standing in the middle of the
road.

Woman With A Tiara   Is he unconscious?

Police 4   Get his legs. Put the right wrist on first.

Helicopter Boy   I need my pen. I need my mum. Where's my mum? Where's my mum?

Girl With No Shoes   I have to say that you're not listening to me.

Police 2   I am listening to you.

Girl With No Shoes   Nobody's listening to me.

Girl With Sparkles   Can you see me? Can you see me? Can you see me dancing?

Brother   I've never seen police crying before.

Sister   He's not crying.

Brother   He is.

Sister   I'm getting bored now.

Brother   Should we go?

Sister   Let's go.

Police 1   Michael.

Police 2   His face. His face is just fucked.

Girl Who Sparkles   We could do whatsits face. 'Auld Lang Syne'. Should we do that?

Police 4   Madam, whereabouts are you from? What's your country of origin?

Girl With No Shoes   What has that got to do with anything?

Police 4   There's no need to be aggressive.

Girl With No Shoes   I'm not being aggressive.

Police 4   If you continue with this line of aggression we may be forced to take further steps.

Girl Who Sparkles   'Should auld acquaintance be forgot' –

Police 1   Constable. Pull yourself together.

Police 2   I can't bear this.

Woman With A Tiara   I am watching you. I am watching you. I can see everything. You are so fucked. I'm going to get the numbers on your badges. I'm going to find out who you are. I'm going to find out where you live. I am going to take this to the government. I am going to take this to the highest court in the fucking country. I am going to stop this from happening. Here. Now. This kind of thing can't happen any more. I am going to stop it. Me.

Man In Blue   I'm nearly there. I can hold it. I can pick it up. I can. I can. I will. I can. I can.

*

Man In Blue   Shhh. Look. Up there. In the sky. You can see it.

And if you listen. Quietly. Carefully.

You can hear the whole world.

At the bottom of the well.

This is what nobody knows. There is a well on Well Street. It has been buried and covered up for hundreds of years.

It goes two hundred feet under the ground. And if you put your ear to the ground you can hear all the voices of all of the people who have ever lived in this city and ever died here.

They're down there.

They're so happy.

And up there. If you lie on your back. And close your eyes. You can see thousands and thousands of miles into the future.

The stars in the skies have burnt up and died. It has just taken millions and millions of years for their light to get here. And

if you go on to those stars. And look back down on the Earth.
The things you will see happened thousands of years ago. So
somewhere in space everything that has ever happened on
this planet is still happening. And somewhere, in space,
everything that will ever happen has happened. And if you lie
like this you can see it.

It's beautiful. Leave me. Quiet now. I don't regret anything
any more. There. Just there. Just like that. Just there.

*

Police 4   I can't believe you were fucking crying.

Police 2   I wasn't crying.

Police 4   You were howling like a fucking cat.

Police 2   I wasn't saying anything.

Police 4   You pissed yourself.

Police 2   I didn't.

Police 4   You fucking shat yourself.

Police 2   You're imagining things.

Police 4   You fucking shat your pants and cried like an
animal.

Police 2   You're imagining the smell of shit. Does it follow
you everywhere?

Police 3   Come on, you two. Please just give it a break.

Police 4   He's a fucking crying weeping pissing shitting
shell of a policeman and he should be ashamed of himself.

Police 2   I'm not.

Police 4   He should be.

Police 2   I shouldn't.

Police 4   He should be down on his knees begging for me to say it's all right.

Police 1   Give it a break yeah?

Police 4   I'm sorry, Constable?

Police 1   It's New Year's Eve.

Police 4   I'm aware of that, mate.

Police 1   We've got a long night ahead of us.

Police 4   My favourite night of the year, this.

Police 1   We may as well try and get it over and done with.

Police 4   I love the noise of it. I love the smell of it. I love the way the boys all buff themselves up with their muscles and their nicest shirt and the girls put on their make-up and flash a graze of tit and a touch of lace at the top of their thigh and the bars are pumping and the music's pumping and the city's pumping and the cars are roaring.

And the sirens are blaring and my adrenaline is on full charge and I am never stopping. Not now. This is my night. This is my year. I'm just fucking getting going.

Helicopter Boy   I can taste blood.

Police 4   It's pouring down your face.

Helicopter Boy   Where are you taking me?

Police 4   You're coming with us.

Helicopter Boy   Where though?

Police 4   We're going down to the station.

Helicopter Boy   Am I going to jail now?

Police 4   For years and fucking years.

Helicopter Boy   Do you think I'm scared?

Police 2   I honestly have no idea.

Helicopter Boy   Do you think I'm scared of what's going to happen? Do you think I'm scared of the New Year? Everything is going to change round here. You are, all of you, fucked. The freaks are taking over. The cunts are taking over. The homos are taking over. The trannies are taking over. The queers are taking over.

Police 3   What the fuck?

Helicopter Boy   The dead are taking over.

Police 2   The dead?

Helicopter Boy   You know what's going to happen this year? With the money. And the food and the smells and the sewers. The people underneath the ground and the dead are going to rise up and God is going to disappear and everything's going to disappear and all of it and the sound and the throb and it's not stopping none of it. None of it is stopping now.

*

Girl Who Sparkles   I didn't mean it.

Girl With No Shoes   You did.

Girl Who Sparkles   Sometimes you say things just for the sake of saying them.

Girl With No Shoes   Not things like that you don't.

Girl Who Sparkles   I do.

Girl With No Shoes   Well you should talk to somebody about that.

Girl Who Sparkles   It's cos I'm tired.

Girl With No Shoes   We're all fucking tired. We don't go round calling people who we are meant to like names like 'fat cunt'.

Girl Who Sparkles   I've been working all day. I've been drinking since midday.

Girl With No Shoes   You called me a 'fat cunt' and you said my neck stank.

Girl Who Sparkles   I know. I said I'm sorry.

Girl With No Shoes   Firstly. I'm not sure 'sorry' covers it because that is just horrible and it was really upsetting, especially when I really liked that boy and he seemed really interested in my work and coming over and saying 'Don't listen to her she's a fat cunt and her neck stinks' is just horrible. Especially after he asked me who you were and I had to say you were my best friend.

Girl Who Sparkles   I know, right.

Girl With No Shoes   And secondly, of all the parts of my body that smell a bit. How do you know it's just my neck?

Girl Who Sparkles   I've no idea.

Girl With No Shoes   Don't say it like that.

Girl Who Sparkles   Like what?

Girl With No Shoes   Like I'm being horrible.

Girl Who Sparkles   I wasn't trying to.

Girl With No Shoes   And have you seen?

Girl Who Sparkles   What?

Girl With No Shoes   The colour of that boy's sick.

Girl Who Sparkles   Oh my God.

Girl With No Shoes   I don't think we should be sitting here.

Girl Who Sparkles   I know.

Girl With No Shoes   Not when there is sick which is actually that colour on the actual floor.

Girl Who Sparkles   Is he all right?

Girl With No Shoes   I don't know.

Girl Who Sparkles   He's not moved.

Girl With No Shoes   Hey. Mister.

Girl Who Sparkles   He's quite handsome.

Girl With No Shoes   Mister. Are you all right?

Girl Who Sparkles   He's got very beautiful cheekbones.

Girl With No Shoes   Would you like us to call somebody for you?

Girl Who Sparkles   But he is shivering.

Girl With No Shoes   We could call a doctor.

Girl Who Sparkles   His leg is really trembling.

Girl With No Shoes   Or your friends.

Girl Who Sparkles   It's making the whole fence shake. The whole building.

Girl With No Shoes   Where have your friends gone? Those girls? Or if there's anybody else we could call for you. Is there anybody else we could call for you?

Girl Who Sparkles   I don't think he can hear us.

Girl With No Shoes   By the look of it he can't hear anything.

Girl Who Sparkles   Is he crying?

Girl With No Shoes   No.

Girl Who Sparkles   Is he asleep? Standing up?

Girl With No Shoes   No.

Girl Who Sparkles   I'm really sorry.

Girl With No Shoes   I know.

Girl Who Sparkles   I didn't mean anything.

Girl With No Shoes   I know. I think I'm going to go.

Girl Who Sparkles   I thought you would. I might make sure he's okay.

Girl With No Shoes   I thought you'd do that too.

*

Police 2   Where are you from, sweetheart?

The Woman Who Can See Under The World   What's that got to do with anything?

Police 2   I'm just thinking about how we're going to get you home.

The Woman   I don't need to get home.

Police 1   Are you not cold, love?

The Woman   I'm not your love.

Police 1   I didn't mean that.

The Woman   I'm not your love and I'm not his sweetheart.

Police 2   We could even put you in the van. Give you a lift. It's not like you've bothered anybody.

Police 1   We're just a bit worried.

Police 2   I'm very worried.

The Woman   What are you worried about?

Police 2   The man in the shop said you'd been here for two hours staring into the wall.

The Woman   I'm not staring into the wall.

Police 1   Are you not?

The Woman   No.

Police 2   What are you doing then, sweetheart?

The Woman   Will you stop calling me that please?

Police 2   I'm sorry. I don't mean to –

The Woman   I'm looking down there.

Police 2   Down there?

The Woman   Can you see?

Police 2   Where?

The Woman   There.

Look.

Police 1   I'm really sorry, Miss. We've got blankets in the van. If you can come with us we can get you warmed up and the Duty Sergeant always has a brew on and he can make you some tea and we can find out where we need to get you to and make sure you get there.

The Woman   Look.

Police 2   Down here?

The Woman   In the hole.

Police 2   Okay.

Jesus.

Police 1   What?

Police 2   Is that?

Police 1   What?

Police 2   Is that what I think it is?

The Woman   I told you.

Police 1   What is it?

Police 2   Who are they?

The Woman   My dad's down there.

Police 2   When did he –?

The Woman   Four years ago.

Police 2   Is my brother down there?

The Woman   I don't know.

Police 2   They look so happy.

The Woman   Are they still dancing?

Police 2   Yeah. They are! Yeah.

Police 1   Michael –

Police 2   It's unbelievable.

Police 1   Michael, are you okay?

Police 2   I'm looking for my brother, David.

The Woman   You can't see them in any of the other holes. It's just that one.

Police 2   Where are they?

The Woman   I don't know. It looks good though, doesn't it?

Police 2   It looks lovely.

Police 1   Michael, what is it?

Police 2   You can't look.

Police 1   Michael?

Police 2   She can look again but you're not getting a look. It's just for us. David! David! I see him. Can he see me?

The Woman   No.

Police 2   Have you tried calling?

The Woman   All night.

Police 2   David. David. David.

Police 1   Are we going to take this woman home?

The Woman   I can't leave.

Police 2   No.

We can't leave.

I'm not going anywhere.

*

Girl With Trainers   I am not sorry for pissing on the street.

I am not sorry for pissing on your shop.

I'm not sorry for pissing on your burgers and fried chicken.

I am not sorry for pissing on the flag of your country.

I am not sorry for pissing on the United States of America.

I am not sorry about you seeing my vagina.

I am not sorry for my vagina in any way.

I am not sorry about my body.

I'm not sorry about my brain.

I'm not sorry about the things that I said.

I'm not sorry about the things that I wrote.

I am not sorry about the things I put on Twitter.

I'm not sorry about the things I said about your country.

Or the things that I did to your country.

Or my granddad did to your country.

Or the things that my country did to your country.

I'm not sorry your country is fucked. Or that the money has run out in your country. Or that there are people there doing terrible things. I'm not sorry about the firebombs or the gang rapes or the female circumcision or the water drought or use of Sarin or the use of mustard gas or the unlawful detainment

that has gone on in your country. Or for setting fire to the
refugee camps. Or firebombing the hospitals. Or blowing up
the peace envoys. Or taking all your food. Or spraying all
your crops with Novichok nerve agents. Or firebombing your
TV stations. Or firebombing your comedians. Or shooting
your comedians. Or executing your rock stars. Live. On telly.
I am not sorry about that. They deserved it. You deserved it.
You fucking deserved it.

*

Woman With A Bag   If I close my eyes none of this will
be real.

If I close my eyes she won't have said anything.

If I close my eyes that boy won't be shaking there and sick.

Nobody will know I've been out to the club.

They won't have seen me on any cameras.

Nobody will recognise me.

Only computers recognise people now. I definitely don't.

Get back home.

Go to sleep.

Get up early.

Go for a run.

Have a shower. Get some breakfast.

Get to the office.

I can work on New Year's Day. That's not bad. That's good.

The start of a new year.

*

Ralph Lauren   I keep dreaming.

I'm not tired. Don't tell me to go to sleep because I'm not tired.

I can't get that tune out of my head. 'Looking back to when we first met. I cannot escape and I cannot forget.'

If I stay here will my toothache go away? If I stay here will my back start to feel better? If I stay here will the noises stop? If I stay here will the ocean get smaller?

The taste of wine. The feeling of raspberries on my tongue. The smell of her perfume. The sound of his laugh. The feeling of falling. The sound of music at Christmas. The sound that an email has arrived on my phone. The feeling that the Earth is spinning. The energy of the Earth spinning. The Earth is spinning.

*

Vijay   We could go to Paris.

Maria   I've never been.

Vijay   It's the most beautiful city in the world. It's romantic. We can drink red wine and smoke cigarettes and eat croissants.

Maria   That sounds beautiful.

Vijay   And we could go to India. I'd take you to where my grandmother comes from.

Maria   What's India like?

Vijay   It's a very complicated place. There's so many people there. It's huge. The mountains are amazing.

Maria   And the food.

Vijay   Yeah. The food's pretty great.

Maria   It's gonna be our year.

Vijay   I think it really could be.

Maria   Tell me your name again.

Vijay   Vijay.

Maria   Like Vijay the DJ.

Vijay   That's right.

Maria   Are you actually a DJ?

Vijay   No.

Maria   What are you?

Vijay   I'm a law student.

Maria   At the university?

Vijay   That's right.

Maria   So are you gonna be like a lawyer?

Vijay   I am, yeah.

Maria   Fuck.

Vijay   I'm going to be so like a lawyer that I am actually going to be a lawyer.

Maria   You're gonna be pretty fucking rich if you're going to be a lawyer.

Vijay   Yeah baby.

Maria   That's good. That'd be great, that.

Vijay   I know.

Maria   I'm fucking sick of being skint me.

I'm skint all the time. I always have been.

It does my head in. Makes me want to fucking go crazy.

What will you buy me?

Vijay   What would you like me to buy you?

Maria   With your lawyer money.

Vijay   I'll buy you anything you want.

Maria   Flowers.

Vijay   A hundred roses. Every day.

Maria   And diamonds.

Vijay   I will put a diamond on every part of your body.

Maria   Every part?

Vijay   Every part.

Maria   You dirty bastard.

Vijay   My friend, you have no idea.

Maria   And clothes.

Vijay   Anything you want.

Maria   A house.

Vijay   In Paris?

Maria   Or India.

Vijay   Or both.

Maria   A plane.

Vijay   Your own plane?

Maria   Yeah.

Vijay   You want your own plane?

Maria   Yes I do, please.

Vijay   All right. Your wish is my command.

Maria   Vijay.

Vijay   Maria.

Maria   I'm not drunk any more.

Vijay   Me neither.

Maria   I kind of mean it.

Vijay   Me too.

Maria   I don't mean about the plane. Or about the money. Or any of that. Or even about Paris. Just about the bit about being sick of being poor.

Vijay   I know.

Maria   I just want a bit more just for a bit.

Vijay   I know.

Maria   It would be all right, wouldn't it?

Vijay   I think it would.

Maria   We'd be all right. Don't you think?

Vijay   I do.

Maria   I do too.

Vijay   I do three.

Maria   I do four.

*

Police 1   How long we got left now?

Police 3   This is the last one, I reckon.

Police 1   Should we all go?

Police 4   Back of the van. Don't put his seat belt on. Accelerate around the corners.

Police 1   See how long before he starts crying.

Police 4   See how long before he fucking throws up.

Police 3   Harsh she is. Isn't she?

Police 1   She has no mercy. No pity. A cold cold heart.

Police 3   He's a poor sod.

Police 4   His arse fucking stinks.

Police 1   Has he shat himself?

Police 4   I am not getting in the back of the van if he has fucking shat himself.

Police 1   Been a night, hasn't it?

Police 3   Not too bad.

Police 1   Getting better round here I reckon.

You should have seen it fifteen years ago.

Police 4   Here we go.

Police 1   Tonight is nothing compared to then. I'm telling you.

It's the world.

Police 3   What about it?

Police 1   Getting better.

Police 4   Is it fuck getting better.

Police 1   It is though.

Police 4   Are you stupid?

Police 1   No.

Police 4   It's fucked.

Police 1   Not as fucked is my point.

Police 4   The world is fucking shafted.

Police 1   It isn't. We think that it is but that's just our brains.

Police 4   The ecology is fucked. The economy's fucked. The terrorists are coming. There's too many people. There's nowhere for them to fucking go any more.

Police 1   Is one way of looking at it.

Police 3   God, he's sleepy this one, isn't he? Is he actually asleep?

Police 1   On the other hand.

People are living longer. Diseases are disappearing. Poverty is disappearing. People are working less. Eating more. Eating better. The death rate is declining. Child labour is declining. Capital punishment is declining.

Police 3   Have you called the station? Told them we're bringing this boy in?

Police 1   Violent crime is declining. More people are able to vote than ever before. People are better educated than ever before. IQ is rising. War is fading away.

What? It's true.

For the first time in history there's no war in the Western world.

Police 4   It's not the Western world we're fucking worried about. Is it? It's the fucking, the fucking, the fucking, the others.

Police 3   Jesus. That was a yawn.

Police 4   I'm fucking fucked.

Police 3   You on tomorrow?

Police 4   Nah. Two days off.

Police 1   What you gonna do?

Police 4   Fucking. Sleep. I reckon.

Right. Head down, sunshine. You got the cuffs, Constable?

Police 1   Yes Ma'am.

Police 4   You all right, lad?

Redhead Boy   Where am I?

Police 4   We're in the centre of town lad. We're just on Well Street. It's New Year's Eve. And we're taking you in. You're coming with us.

*

Brother   Are you not exhausted?

Sister   I'm fine.

Brother   Are you sure?

Sister   What do you mean 'are you sure'?

Brother   It's really late.

Sister   I know. So. Stop going on about it.

Brother   I know what you get like.

Sister   I'm not even that sleepy.

Brother   But you will be.

Sister   Have you heard yourself?

Brother   We should go home.

Sister   You're worse than Dad.

Brother   I'm right though.

Sister   I don't want to go home. Not tonight. Not ever. I'm tired of going home. All we ever do is go home. I'm sick of it. I'm never fucking going home ever again.

Brother   That's a bit extreme.

Sister   Do you think I don't mean it?

Brother   It's been the most amazing night.

Sister   Yes. It really has. It has.

Brother   Are you sure you're sure?

Sorry.

Do you think that means it's going to be an amazing New Year?

*

Girl With Trainers   You all right?

Woman With A Bag   Have you got her?

Girl With Trainers   Course I have.

Woman With A Bag   She's nearly strangling me. Where did you find her?

Girl With Trainers   She was by the wall. Staring into the pavement.

Woman With A Bag   She's all right, aren't you? Hey? Are you all right?

Woman Who Can See Under The World   I'm fine.

Woman With A Bag   You're not gonna be sick are you?

Woman Who Can See Under The World   No.

Woman With A Bag   I'm tired of people being sick all over me.

Woman Who Can See Under The World   I'm not gonna be sick, right.

Woman With A Bag   You better not be.

Girl With Trainers   Let's just get her home.

Woman With A Bag   My feet are absolutely killing me.

Girl With Trainers   Should we get an Uber?

Woman With A Bag   Fucking surge prices. Fucking twenty-five-minute wait.

Woman Who Can See Under The World   Who are all those people?

Girl With Trainers   What people?

Woman Who Can See Under The World   That lot. They're all looking at me.

Girl With Trainers   They're not.

Woman Who Can See Under The World   They are. I can tell.

Girl With Trainers   Don't pay any attention to them.

Woman Who Can See Under The World   I'll fucking have them.

Girl With Trainers   No you won't. You can barely stand up.

Woman With A Bag   You are not starting anything now.

Woman Who Can See Under The World   It's very bright isn't it?

Girl With Trainers   What is?

Woman Who Can See Under The World   The light?

Girl With Trainers   It is a bit.

Woman Who Can See Under The World   Is it shining on us?

Girl With Trainers   No. It's just the light from the shop.

Woman Who Can See Under The World   Is it a searchlight?

Girl With Trainers   No. It's the light from the shop so that people can see their kebabs.

Woman Who Can See Under The World   Is it a police helicopter?

Girl With Trainers   Why would a police helicopter be looking for you?

Woman Who Can See Under The World   I don't know.

They do that kind of thing though, don't they? Fucking police. They're always after people.

Girl With Trainers   They're not.

Woman Who Can See Under The World   They fucking are. Fucking wankers.

She sings to the tune of 'Ring a Ring of Roses'.

All the cops are wankers! All the cops are wankers!

Woman With A Bag   My Uncle Michael's a cop. He's not a wanker.

Woman Who Can See Under The World   He is.

Woman With A Bag   He's all right.

Woman Who Can See Under The World   He's a fucking wanker.

Oh.

Girl With Trainers   What?

Woman Who Can See Under The World   Just a burp.

Woman With A Bag   It better had be.

Woman Who Can See Under The World   It is. I'm fine. It's gone.

I could kill a kebab right now.

Girl With Trainers   I've not got any money left.

Woman With A Bag   Nobody has.

Girl With Trainers   What should we do tomorrow?

Woman Who Can See Under The World   New Year!

Woman With A Bag   I know.

Woman Who Can See Under The World   Happy New Year! Happy New Year! Happy New Year! 'Should auld acquaintance be forgot. And never come to rise! We'll drink a cup of kindness yet. For the sake of Auld Lang Syne.'

Woman With A Bag   Will somebody shut her up?

Thank you.

Girl With Trainers   Fucking. Sleep. Go for a walk. Go and see the world. I honestly have no idea.

For a complete listing of
Methuen Drama titles, visit:
www.bloomsbury.com/drama

Follow us on Twitter and keep up to date
with our news and publications
@MethuenDrama